If you desire to journey closer to the heart of the Father, *Throne Room Prayers* will draw you in. Through sharing her personal experience, Dr. Biltz tutors us in biblical principles and prayer techniques which help us to gain intimacy with God and insight into His will for our lives. I recommend this book to pastors, teachers, small group leaders and spiritual directors, or any Christian who is in a process of discovery about who they are in Christ.

Rev. Valerie G. Schubert
Pastor-Developer, The Dwelling Place
Spiritual Counselor, VNA Hospice, Inc.

Throne Room
PRAYERS

A manual on how to get your
prayers answered

Saundra Biltz

WestBow
PRESS
A DIVISION OF THOMAS NELSON

WestBow Press books may be ordered through booksellers or by contacting:

WestBow Press
A Division of Thomas Nelson
1663 Liberty Drive
Bloomington, IN 47403
www.westbowpress.com
1-(866) 928-1240

Edited by Nia Austin

ISBN: 978-1-4497-9064-6 (sc)
ISBN: 978-1-4497-9063-9 (e)

Library of Congress Control Number: 2013906126

Printed in the United States of America.

WestBow Press rev. date: 4/8/2013

Table of Contents

Dedication

I dedicate this book to my warrior sisters in the *Living Faith Bible Study* group, a covenant group started by the Holy Spirit at our place of worship, *Covenant Church of Pittsburgh*, where Bishop Joseph Garlington is the senior pastor. We faithfully met at the local *Panera Bread* restaurant every other Wednesday for a season, sometimes just barely making it there. We all had hurried and busy lives, showing up oftentimes with battle fatigue from challenging days at work and at home. Once there though, the Holy Spirit would show up and sometimes show out.

I list the names of the Father's warriors in training in no particular order: Bettina Nickens, Christina Thomas, Renee Melton, Tracey Williams, Delilah Harper and Kelly Smithson. We have been put together for such a time as this to learn how to do battle for the kingdom. You have been instrumental in sharpening my teaching skills and helping me to better articulate what the Lord has put on my heart in regards to prayer. My assignment for the group was to allow it to be a training ground for women to practice their spiritual gifts in a loving and safe environment. I did not expect that it would become a training ground for me to write a book. *Throne Room Prayer* is a direct result of our time together; I thank God that it will bless your socks off!

Introduction

Throughout my Christian walk I was often puzzled at what seemed to be the lack of answers to my prayers. I could not understand why my time in prayer would often produce meager fruit. Not only were my own prayers fruitless, but also the prayers of those whom I thought to be more spiritually mature than I. I knew His Word said that "the effective, fervent prayer of a righteous man avails much" (James 5:16), but at times I was not seeing significant results from time spent in my prayer closet. I went through all the proper techniques that I had been taught over the years; making sure I had repented of any sin, practicing the PUSH (pray until something happens) prayer, etc. but I intuitively felt something was not quite right.

I felt like I was fighting an uphill battle trying to get God to change something in my life. It seemed to me, that I had gotten similar results by pushing through obstacles in my own strength in the natural.

In Bible school we learned all about the fundamentals of prayer, as well as the posture and attitude of praying fervently. Praying in the spirit has proven to be very powerful and it remains to be my go-to prayer stance, but something happened once while praying in the spirit that began to change my approach to prayer. I began to spontaneously interpret what the Holy Spirit was saying in my natural language. It doesn't happen all the time, but this experience began to open me up to a better way to pray using my natural language.

Then in July of 2012, my husband and I took a trip to Canada for our 7th anniversary. Even though Canada was not our first choice, it was a relatively quick and inexpensive trip, and turned out to be a pivotal event in my spiritual journey. We visited *Catch The Fire* church, the home of the *Toronto Airport* revival. There the Holy Sprit led me to the teachings of one of my spiritual mentors. I could not believe that what I was reading in his books was exactly what I was just beginning to learn in the spirit, and some of it was written 10 years prior! Now keep in mind, I had completed Bible school and was a licensed minister before I even realized there was much more to prayer than I had been taught!

In this book I will share with you some of the things the Holy Spirit put on my heart regarding prayer. It all boils down to praying from who we are in Christ. I will attempt to do justice to this topic, but if after reading this book you are interested in a deeper dive, please visit Graham Cooke's website at www.brilliantbooks.com. Graham Cooke is a brilliantly anointed general in God's army and a much more eloquent writer than I.

It is my prayer that reading this book will ignite a desire in you to pray prayers from the *Throne Room* and co-labor with the Father, the Son and the Holy Spirit to usher in the kingdom of God on earth, as it is in heaven.

CHAPTER 1

What is Throne Room Prayer?

But seek ye first the kingdom of God,
and His righteousness;
and all these things shall be added unto you.
Matthew 6:33

Throne room prayer, is prayer that is crafted from a majestic viewpoint. It is the type of prayer that makes our God bigger than any and every circumstance or situation that is placed before you. When we think about a throne room we think about a majestic place in heaven where the Father abides. We get the sense of a place in time and space outside of ourselves. We may even imagine in our mind's eye a picture as depicted in John's vision in the book of Revelation. However, the Father, by His Holy Spirit abides in all of us, so let me suggest to you that you have access to the throne room when you attune your whole heart and your whole mind toward the Father. In that sense, we can meet the Father in the throne room of our hearts, and that can be done anywhere, when we sit and focus our attention on the Father and His majesty.

The throne room seen from this perspective, is then not only about a far away mystical place. It then becomes a very present and authentic space where we can meet the Father, right here and right now in the throne room of our hearts and minds, in which He also resides.

Throne room prayer is about covering everything with the majesty of the Father. It is the type of prayer that Jesus used to feed the multitude, Elijah used to stop the rain, and the early church used to miraculously free Peter from jail. Throne room prayer, is setting into motion on earth the activities that are happening in heaven. It is doing our part in preparing the way for the supernatural to come into the natural.

Throne room prayer simply believes God at His Word. It requires belief in the dominion, power, authority and majesty of the Father. Everything about God is majestic. Majesty is an English word derived from the Latin word *maiestas,* meaning "greatness." We serve a great God who is able to do exceedingly and abundantly above all that we can ask or think (Ephesians 3:20-21)! Sadly, many Christians in the Western church come to God with prayers from a limited, earthbound perspective. We often recite prayers that give the enemy more power then the Father. We use earthbound logic and reasoning to try to get the Father to do something for us. We pray from a stance of defeat trying to gain victory over a situation or circumstance. We often want God to rescue us, failing to see that He already rescued us when He nailed His Son to the cross.

We do not rise up to a majestic view of prayer because we do not understand the kingdom in which we reside. Not only that, we do not understand our role in the kingdom, which is to co-operate with the Holy Spirit as sons and daughters in Christ.

That is a shame because Jesus took much effort and trying to teach us what the kingdom of God is all about. In fact, that was the entirety of His message! He came to set the captives free from the religious mindset of the day. He presented to us many parables explaining the Kingdom of Heaven to help us understand that the kingdom is the primary thing—not religion, not rules, not procedures.

Part of understanding the kingdom involves understanding our role in the kingdom. It is about understanding who we are in relationship to the Father. Once we truly recognize and accept our son-ship and our inheritance in Christ, we begin to realize that we have permission granted to take ground for the kingdom. It is our birthright. Out of relationship comes responsibility. We begin to come boldly to the throne, not as orphans begging for bread, but as much loved sons and daughters of the Father declaring His word in faith to accomplish His will.

But you see, you have to know what His will is. How can you do that? Spend time in His presence. Rest in Him and get to know His character. Ask the Holy Spirit to teach you about His nature. The Father loves it when we want to get to know Him better.

Start with love. Get to know the love of the Father. Let His love fill you up. It's not as difficult as you may think. The resistance that you may feel in getting to know Him better has nothing to do with Him. Oftentimes it is just fear because you are doing something new. It may be the selfish part of you wanting all the attention to be focused on yourself. Or you may feel unworthy to be in His presence because of past-present sin in your life. Whatever it is, just decide to get over yourself. When we come to the Father we are clothed in His righteousness, not ours. It is a gift and it is our inheritance.

As you begin to just seek Him more, without your list of prayer requests, He will begin to reveal more of Himself to you. As a few of my teachers have said, "as it is in the spirit, so it is in the natural." When you are getting to know someone in the natural, you show an interest in him or her, just for who they are. You have no hidden agenda to figure out what they can do for you. You just want to love them and be loved by them. It is a time of enjoyment.

When I first talk to people about spending more time in His presence, they often say they are too busy or they feel awkward just sitting there. They also say their mind wanders. I tell them, that it's okay. God is still there even when your mind is wandering. He is also still there in the awkward silence. We have gotten so accustomed to performing and or striving for His approval we often think we have to be doing something; otherwise the time we spend with Him doesn't count. With the Father it is always about the intentions of the heart. The Holy Spirit can still do a great work in your heart even when your mind is not completely engaged in the process. When you begin to understand how much He loves you even though your mind wanders, or even though you may fall asleep, you relax more. You no longer view it as yet another chore on your already overwhelming to-do list. In fact, you may even start to enjoy it.

So I urge you to begin to sit with Him, just to be with Him, or to seek His face. Spend time simply being still and knowing that God is God (Psalm. 46:10).

CHAPTER 2

How to Prepare Yourself for Throne Room Prayer

But as it is written, Eye has not seen, nor ear heard,
Nor have entered into the heart of man, the things
which God has prepared for those who love Him.
1 Corinthians 2:9

Once while journaling during my own prayer time, I heard the Father say in my spirit, "There are some things about Me that you believe that are not truth." At that time I had recently become licensed as a minister of the gospel, and He was telling me that I was still holding onto beliefs about Him that were not true! It hurt my feelings at first, and then I got over it and asked the Holy Spirit to show me which thoughts about the Father I needed to change. In asking that question I don't think I was prepared for the magnificence of the revelation about His nature that I would receive.

As the weeks and months went by He showed me different aspects of His majesty. I was overwhelmed by His goodness,

His loving-kindness, His joy, His peace and His friendship with me. How did He do that? He used my everyday ordinary circumstances; in fact, he used every aspect of my life—the good, the bad and the ugly—to show me His unfailing presence. He began to allow me to see things from His perspective.

In an open vision He took me to the ledge of a mountain and allowed me to see, symbolically, all the things that were going on in my life, even the hidden traps. He gave me this panoramic view from above and told me that I no longer live in my circumstances. I am seated far above with Christ in heavenly places. He wanted me to live from this ascended place and not get caught up in circumstances. In order to do that I needed to confront some issues in my life that I thought I had already dealt with. The first was a poverty spirit. The conversation went something like this:

> Father: *I am removing from you a poverty spirit.*

> Me: *I still have a poverty spirit? I thought I gotten rid of that along time ago.* (Note: I did not waste any time being offended. Progress had been made.)

> Father: *A poverty spirit is not only a deficiency in your finances, but also a deficiency in your thinking that trickles down into the natural realm. A poverty spirit*

is a spirit that accepts only meager possibilities, meager
rewards, meager ambitions, meager everything.

Me: *What is it about your fullness of goodness,*
blessings and favor that I am afraid of? Why do I
only seem to be able to accept a portion or a measure
of what you have for me?

This back and forth went on for a few minutes and then I was given a vision of a rebellious teenager. You know, the kind of situation where all you are trying to do is to help this person and you want the best for them, but because of some inner wounding they are not able to receive it. So they act out, or they may even reject you. Well, that is how we are sometimes, even as adults. He allowed me to see that because of wounds from past experiences I was not able to receive all that He had for me. I needed to stop living in my past–present, and to begin to live in my present–future in order to be able to receive the help I needed.

He also gave me a vision of someone drowning. In that picture, a lifeguard was trying to save someone's life. You know how a person will sometimes flail and fight against the lifeguard even though s/he is there to save one's life? The lifeguard just needs the person to remain calm and let him do his work and get him/her to safety. The same is true in the spirit. Often times my approach to prayer had been this weeping and gnashing of teeth to help save my life, so to speak, but He was telling me I didn't need to do that. I could come to Him with quiet assurance that He had already saved me from whatever disaster I thought was about to strike. I just needed to remain calm, and rest in His arms, with confidence as He brought me safely to shore.

When you finally let go of the poverty spirit you no longer kick against the goad, because you no longer view yourself as unworthy. You know that you are a much- loved child of the most high God. Much loved children don't worry about anything, they know their parents will take care of them no matter what. They are safe and secure in the fact that they are much loved. Jesus says in (Matthew 7:11), *"if you then, being evil, know how to give good gifts to your children, how much more will your Father who is in heaven give good things to those who ask Him!"*

My previous conversation with the Father ended something like this:

> Father: *I want to give you everything but you are fighting me. You are fighting against what I have already given you.*
>
> Me: *I know, and thank you for loving me still. Thank you for teaching me to rest in your presence and showing me how to co-operate with Your Holy Spirit.*

In preparing yourself for throne room prayer, there may be some beliefs about the Father, and your relationship to Him that you may have to give up. It's not always easy to give up cherished thoughts we have, even if they happen to be lies. Sometimes we make idols of our thoughts and they become strongholds.

You must acknowledge who He is and who you are. Not just by making a mental assent of this information but knowing in your heart of hearts that you have an inheritance in Christ. Depending on where you are on your spiritual walk, it may take some time to begin to understand, and then begin to walk out your identity in Christ. Until then, you may have trouble with this level of prayer, because what you ask for and how you ask for it is intimately connected to how you view and relate to the Father.

The poverty spirit was not the only thing the Father had to get out of me before I could approach Him with boldness and confidence. He is still doing a work in me with regard to receiving all that He has for me. Although it is not easy, it is critical to go through the process of weeding out the negative attitudes and personifications we have about ourselves and about our God, as we continue to move forward in the spirit.

In addition to the poverty spirit, here are more examples of negativity in spirit and attitude that may limit the effectiveness of your prayer life:

- Feelings of unworthiness
- Fear
- Anxiety
- Timidity
- Excessive self-consciousness
- Rejection
- An orphan spirit

The list could go on and on. To figure out what limits you personally, ask the Holy Spirit to reveal the areas of negativity that you must give up in order to consistently and effectively pray before the Father's throne. Listen for what He says, even if it seems to make no sense to you or, if it is something that you thought that you had dealt with long ago. Honor the revelation that comes and repent, when necessary, to move through the process.

Exercise 1

Ask the Holy Spirit, "What negative aspects of my personality and attitude prevent me from coming to the Father as a much loved son/ daughter?"

Sit with the question and just wait awhile. It is okay if you are uncomfortable with sitting and waiting. Be uncomfortable and do it anyway. Whatever He reveals to you, thank Him for it because it needs to be revealed in order to be healed. It is already done in the heavenlies; it is now to be done in the natural. In exchange for the pain that may surface as you go through this process, His promise is to fill you with His joy.

Once the negative attitudes are revealed, then it is time to do some work. Allow Him to speak into those areas for you. Take a few minutes and journal what the Lord wants to reveal to you in the notes section in the back of the book.

If you did not get an impression doing Exercise 1, be okay with that, too. You have asked the question with a pure heart. His Spirit will reveal it to you one way or another, so be on the look out as you go through your day, week, or month. It may come to you while you are driving to work, or in the form of your co-worker, your boss, or your child. I don't know how the Father will choose to reveal it to you, but I can guarantee you, it will be revealed.

The following is a prophetic word the Lord gave to me to help me work through my issues with lack:

Do not be afraid of my immensity. It is not there to intimidate you. It is there to inspire you to be, do and have all that I have for you. I have to be immense as I have much to give. I am giving all the time.

I cannot be depleted. As it is with me so it shall be with you as my spiritual warriors. You have to be able to increase your capacity to give, and in order to do that you have to INCREASE IN ME, yes; you have to have MORE OF ME, which means less of you. But you should be already dead.

Chapter 3

How to Make Your Prayers
More Effective

Enter into His gates with thanksgiving,
And into His courts with praise.
Psalms 100:4

If you have taken the time to do the exercise in the previous chapter, it will help you immensely as you move through the process of renewing your mind. If not, then this book will just wind up being another book on your shelf collecting dust, and you will have missed a tremendous opportunity to transform your thinking.

Exercise 2

Take a sheet of paper and make a list of all the negative traits that He revealed to you in Exercise 1. There may be 5 negative attributes or there may be 27. I had 42 on my initial list. Yes, that's right—there were 42 negative or worldly traits that the Holy Spirit helped me to identify within myself. The number really doesn't matter, but what does matter is the next step. Now if there was no negative trait that was revealed to you, I guess that means you are perfect and there is nothing else for you to learn. I hope you know I was kidding. As long as we are on this side of glory, we will always have something more to learn to become more like our Lord and Savior.

I learned the next step from an audio CD entitled, *Living Your Truest Identity* by Graham Cooke. Take another sheet of paper and ask the Holy Spirit to give you the "opposite" of each trait listed on the negative sheet. For example, you might take "unworthy" from the negative sheet and write the opposite, "worthy," on the positive sheet. The positive trait is your new identity in Christ.

The positive response does not have to be a one-word answer. It can be a sentence, a portion of scripture, or whatever the Holy Spirit gives you. This part is important. We are renaming our old nature and we are staking a claim in the riches of the Father. We are taking our old identity that is full of negative aspects of ourselves from our former sinful nature, which leads to death, and we are replacing them with life-giving statements about who the Father says we are in Christ.

Once you have completed the positive sheet, I want you to tear up or burn the negative sheet. That is no longer who you are. That is your old nature. The word of God states you are a new creation (2nd Corinthians 5:17). When you accepted Jesus Christ as your Lord and Savior, you became a new creature. That old list was your identity in the world or how you were defined by the world. The new list is who you are in Christ in how you are known in heaven.

If you are having trouble with this exercise, take a look in the Appendix A to get a jump-start. I have provided a list of my identity statements in Christ. I don't have the negative list because I burned it! But you will be able to glean from my identity in Christ list, what was on the first list of attributes from my old nature. Make sure you don't just use the words on my list, because you will get much more out of this exercise focusing on what the Holy Spirit is revealing to you about yourself.

The new list, your identity in Christ, is the person you want to be when you come before the throne in prayer. This is how the Father sees you in heaven: redeemed, and made righteous by the blood of the lamb. You can now approach Him in this new identity and, as Matthew 7:7 states, *"Ask, and it will be given to you; seek and you will find; knock and it will be opened."* This should make you ecstatic. You should be jumping up and down with thanksgiving at fact that the Father of all creation has gifted you with His righteousness. You should be full of thanksgiving for this gift that the Father has bestowed on you, and not from anything you could have done to receive it. Not of your works so no man may boast—it is a gift from God (Ephesians 2:8-9).

In order to get this revelation of your identity in Christ you must review your list as often as you think of it. Use a voice recorder to record your identity in Christ and play it back repeatedly. Commit your new identity to memory. Let it get deep into your spirit man.

When you really receive this revelation of how you are known in heaven and get it in your spirit, it becomes revelation knowledge and you begin to live your life from a place of thanksgiving. You begin to thank God for everything in your life, because you know that for every problem, He has already provided you with a promise. He has already provided you with victory over every circumstance because you are his much loved child regardless of how things may appear in the natural.

You are beginning to understand the nature of the Father, which is love, and you are beginning to understand your new nature in Him. Joy and thanksgiving abound!

The secret weapon in throne room prayer is thanksgiving. Come to the Father with thanksgiving for all that He has already accomplished for you in the spirit.

CHAPTER 4

How to Get Your Prayers Answered

"As he thinks in his heart, so is he."
Proverbs 23:7

How do you get your prayers answered? That's simple: Just agree with the Father. It may not be so easy at first. We are so preoccupied with our own wants and needs that it may take some time for that tendency to dissipate. As you begin to just sit in His presence, more and more, His nature will become more familiar to you. You will be able to discern what is you, versus what is Him. Sure, you will make mistakes along the way, but that's part of the training. Ask Him to give you a discerning heart, eyes to see what He is doing and ears to hear what He is saying. As you focus on your new nature, the old nature will start to fall away. The anxiety to get what you want, when you want it and the need for a quick and speedy answer will no longer be your focus. You may be disappointed some days when you feel as if He is not there, but then you'll remember He is always there, because He is inside of you.

Begin to focus on who He says you are. Read scripture to Him. For each problem in your life that you perceive, ask the Holy Spirit to give you the promise that has already been provided for you in His Word.

Remember His Word and His nature will never be in contradiction. He is the same yesterday, today and tomorrow. If you have a thought that is not in His nature, choose another thought. Begin to agree with Him more and more. Read His Word so the Holy Spirit has something to bring to your remembrance. The more time you spend in His presence the more you will begin to see what He sees. How long does this ability take to develop? Well, that depends. When you begin to walk on this path, there is an acceleration that takes place. Don't focus on the result you may be trying to achieve; just focus on seeking His face and it will happen. So what if it takes a couple of months or even a year! You will be better for it, as you are learning to abide in Him and He is adjusting your character to be more closely aligned with His. It is a win–win situation—you cannot lose.

One of the things that will happen while you are learning to rest in Him is that selfishness will begin to fall away. There is no way you can be selfish and be in Christ. Once you figure out that the time you are spending with Him is not for yourself anyway, the urgency fades. Every gift that the Father gives you is for someone else. Your prayers will be less focused on your wants, needs and desires and more focused on what He has already accomplished in heaven. At some point you will find yourself naturally praying the will of the Father because you have spent time learning His nature, and He has spent time transforming your nature and your character to resemble His.

Jesus only did what He saw the Father doing. Beloved, you can attain that same level of intimacy. You may not see with your natural eyes what the Father is doing, but you will know the Fathers' will in the eyes of your heart because He will make it known to you. As you trust Him with more He trusts you with more.

CHAPTER 5

How to Agree with the Father in Prayer

The eyes of your understanding being enlightened;
that you may know what is the hope of His calling,
what are the riches of the glory of His inheritance
in the saints, and what is the exceeding greatness of
His power toward us who believe, according to the
working of His mighty power.

Ephesians 1:18-19

When you are faced with a problem, the best way to approach the Father in prayer, is with the acknowledgement that you are praying from a place of victory. Realize that the battle is already won, according to His sovereign will. There are some things you can just take to the bank, because He has already confirmed His will for His people in His Word. For instance, we know His will is to heal the brokenhearted, proclaim liberty for captives and freedom to prisoners. He wants to comfort those who mourn and give you beauty for ashes. He wants to give us a garment of praise for the spirit of heaviness. This is just a short list. Read the book of Psalms over and over again. Read the gospels. His promises are all throughout the Bible. There is a promise for every single problem that you may encounter.

I believe that we have not trained the eyes of our heart to see what the Father has already accomplished in our lives. We tend to see the circumstance or problem as being the main thing. We focus on the problem and we make it bigger than our promise. An untrained heart will do this. When the eyes of our heart are not focused on the Father, and our identity in Christ we will fall quickly into a "victim of circumstance" mentality, based on former wounds. As Stephen DeSilva states in his book *Money in the Prosperous Soul*, "One of the most powerful skills you can learn as a Christian is to practice a kind of holy denial toward everything that distracts you from fixing your gaze upon Jesus" and I might add, the finished work of the cross.

If you are having a problem agreeing with what the Father has already promised you through His Word, then the problem is not just a belief issue, it is a heart issue. This is where you will need to do further investigation. There is an area in your heart where your relationship with the Father needs to be addressed. For instance, if you cannot come into agreement with the Father in the area of your finances, then you must ask the Holy Spirit to reveal specific events or incidents that may be preventing you from faithfully acknowledging and receiving what God has already provided for you. Somewhere in your logic you are still being held hostage by earthbound thinking and you believe a lie. In terms of finances, the lie could be that you trust money more than you trust God, or that money can make you happier than God can make you. The bottom line is, you may not be trusting that God knows what is best for you in the long run and something is preventing you from seeing the issue from His perspective.

We need to be free from the mental or emotional bondage that keeps us captive in our old nature. Once you identify the issue, you can begin the work of healing. Your journey to wholeness requires courage and the willingness to change. You must allow your heart to soften so that the Holy Spirit can do a work in you, and for some, that process may require the development of additional skills and tools. Some personalities are more open to self-reflection and introspection and such people may be able to work through the process alone. Some of us do better working in a small group format. Determine what works best for you. As a leader in my local congregation I find that most congregants don't take advantage of the help that is available to them through the local church. There are many reasons for this. Some are valid, some are just excuses. The excuse I hear most often is, "I don't want to put my stuff out there", which is obviously a pride or a trust issue. Others say they don't have the time to add yet another meeting to their schedules. My answer to that is to set your priorities in order because you are going pay now or pay later. If you don't put in the work to take up your cross, you will pay for it, if not now, then in eternity. Do something. If you are not growing in Christ, you are backsliding.

If you need more help working through emotional trauma or inner healing, I recommend looking into some form of deliverance ministry in your local church. I personally recommend both *SOZO* inner healing and *Cleansing Streams Ministries*. These ministries are designed to help you walk through your healing with the support of trained individuals. These ministries are strategically put in place at the local church level to assist you with working through issues of the heart, which may be preventing you from operating as a mature son or daughter of the Father. We must learn to take advantage of what is available to us in our local expression of the body of Christ.

In doing the exercises in this book, you have begun the process of this journey into wholeness. The Father honors that. Trust that, if necessary, He will lead you into any additional steps you may need to take, regarding the matter. He wants your heart to be pure so that you can begin to see yourself as He sees you.

We begin to agree with the Father after we have come to the end of wrestling with our identity in Christ. As Jacob wrestled with the angels the night God made a covenant with him (Genesis 28: 10-18), so we must also wrestle with our heart wounds, to be able to walk fully in our identity as mature sons and daughters.

Here is another paradox you should learn to embrace; you are no longer coming to the Father only as a son or daughter, but also as a friend. Once you are able to better identify with your inheritance in Christ, the Father honors that by promoting you, so to speak, to walk in friendship with Him. As a friend of the Father you have a different set of entitlements as well as a different set of responsibilities. For example, you are able to now partner with Him more effectively in His work. Friends confide in each other. God begins to let you in on His plans and His purposes more intimately. You begin to dream with God as opposed to having your own dreams and praying that God blesses your agenda. You dream together, and as you take those steps of faith in co-operation with the Holy Spirit, provision will be provided at every turn.

A young child relates to his parents in a way to get his needs met. As the child gets older the dynamic of that relationship changes. There may now be a "friend" quality added to the relationship because the child is no longer primarily seeking to get their needs met through the parents. A parent of an adult child no longer continues to try to fix their child's problems. They become old enough to join in the family business and help to grow it. As it is in the natural, so it is in the spirit.

In addition to the paradox of the son-friend relationship, there is yet another aspect of our identity that we need to embrace as we mature into all things Christ: our identity as a bride. A bride is a helpmate and a partner to the bridegroom. She knows the longings of the bridegroom's heart and she seeks to help him achieve the desires of his heart because he is the head of the family. She knows that helping him achieve his dreams will automatically take care of the family needs. Her desires and his desires co-mingle and they begin to produce much fruit together. That is what the Father is seeking for us to do: produce much fruit in His name to glorify the kingdom. As a bride you can fully partner with the Father as His helpmate in the natural to bring about what is already occurring in heaven.

Yes, you come before the Father as all three personas, much loved child, friend, and bride just as He comes to us as Father, Son, and Holy Spirit.

CHAPTER 6

Jesus as Our Intercessor

My little children, I write to you these things so that you may not violate God's law and sin. But if anyone should sin, we have an Advocate (One who will intercede for us) with the Father- it is Jesus Christ (the all) righteous (upright, just, who conforms to the Father's will in every purpose, thought and action).

1 John 2:1 (AMP)

When Jesus ascended to the right hand of the Father, He left His role as priest here on earth to take up His role as intercessor for us in heaven. Yes, Jesus is interceding for us at this very moment. He intercedes for us collectively and individually. In *Becoming the Beloved CD*, Graham Cooke tells us to imagine that Jesus is having a conversation with the Father right now about your life. He already knows what you are going through, in fact, the Father has already orchestrated the answer. What we need to do as mature sons and daughters of the Father is enter our prayer time with this truth in mind.

When you are going through a situation or circumstance that may be baffling to you, just sit back and ask the Holy Spirit, "how I can cooperate with the Father and the Son in this situation to get the outcome that the Father has purposed for me?" His plans and purposes are always better then yours. The Father has your best interest in mind. He is not necessarily looking for the quick fix or to get you out of a jam. The Father's agenda is much more holistic. He wants you to see the area of your life that He is trying to bring into alignment with His character and His nature.

There is a throne room prayer exercise that I would like you to complete at the end of this chapter. I will first use an example from my own life as an illustration of how to craft a throne room prayer.

For some reason, the Father most often uses the area of finances in my life, as the hard soil to till the garden of my heart. From this area He has taught me many lessons about His nature regarding His faithfulness (and mine), supernatural provision, security, abundance, prosperity, trust, and patience, just to name a few. I was about to learn a new lesson.

I knew the Lord was taking me through a deeper level of tilling the soil in my heart in the realm of finances. There was another upgrade I needed to experience in order to continue to grow, so that I could handle more of Him. My husband and I found ourselves in an extended state of what I will call an "ebb" season as it related to our household finances. We have gone through "flow" and "ebb" seasons in the past, but this season was lasting a bit longer than usual, and I found myself becoming bewildered and frustrated. That's what got my attention, because I knew that type of frustration was not of the Lord. I also knew we were being obedient with our tithes and offerings, so that wasn't the problem either. I asked the Holy Spirit to reveal any areas of un-confessed sin in our lives—nothing. It just seemed as if everything was drying up. There were hardly any patients coming into my office, and my husband's business was not prospering as well. I finally realized, we were going through an upgrade in the spirit! So I set my mind to see what it was. I sat down in a quiet place, and with the question in my heart, I asked the Father what was going on? What was He trying to teach us at this time, and how could we co-operate in this upgrade with Him?

I heard the Father saying, "I need Saundra to know that even if I gave her what she thinks she needs right now, which is more money, she would not come to know Me as her constant source of joy like I need her to know Me as. She will not see Me as her provider for all things, and as her only source of security. In her heart she still believes it is the amount of money in her bank account that keeps her safe, and she still believes that some of the things that money brings into her life is the source of her contentment. She thinks her problem will be solved and she is partially right. It would be solved in the temporal, but the opportunity for her to experience Me as her source for all things would be lost at this time, and that will hurt her in the long run. It will short circuit the training she is receiving on how to see in the spirit and also what it means to be an extravagant giver. You see, I am training her to be an extravagant giver." He continued, "She needs to know how much I love her and the blessings she receives from Me have more value than anything the world can offer. And she needs to know that with her whole heart."

Then the Holy Spirit reminded me of the story of the widow's gift. Jesus acknowledges this poor widow putting in two cooper coins as well as the rich putting their gifts into the treasury. "So He said, Truly I say to you that this poor widow has put in more than all; for all these out of their abundance have put into the offerings for God, but she out of her poverty put in all the livelihood that she had" (Luke 21: 3-4). He showed me how that was an example of extravagant giving. She was giving out her heart, and it had nothing to do with the amount of money she gave, but it was the condition of her heart that was willing to give all she had.

Even though my husband and I were giving our tenth, and sowing into various ministries, we were still giving out of our surplus, and did not allow our giving to impact our lifestyle very much. It had nothing to do with our normal tithes and offerings that we were currently giving out of obedience to His word. He was showing us a new purpose in giving. He was teaching us to give out of love and compassion, regardless of the effect it had on our lifestyle choices. He was also reminding me that He is a giver. In fact, He is an extravagant giver and we are made in His image. He gives without any fear of lack, and we should do the same. He gives because He loves to give and so should we. My husband and I were encouraged to give much more and live off of much less.

My next step was to immediately write out a prayer that allowed me to agree with what I heard the Father speaking about my life, so that I could do my part in making it a reality on earth. I have included a copy of the *Extravagant Giver* prayer in the Appendix B as an example.

After you go through the process I have outlined for you below, you should be able to see your current circumstances from a more heightened perspective. In my case as we continued to go through our ebb season, we were being consistently challenged to give above and beyond what we had given in the past, even though our income was at its lowest point ever. He would often have us give to individuals or organizations when we barely had enough money to cover our household expenses. You may ask, how did I know it was from the Lord? I knew it was from the Lord because He would put a burden in our hearts with an overwhelming sense of compassion in certain situations that we would normally ignore. We wanted desperately to give these financial gifts as the promptings came, and along with the promptings came this sense of joy and peace that we would still be okay. At first it did not make much sense to our logical minds, but it became easier as we would "hear" the Father's purpose through the prayers that I had written out and recited.

And, by the way, we did not come out of our ebb season immediately; the outer situation had not changed at all. But what had changed was my perspective of it. I'm referring to my perspective and not my husband's because my husband does not have the same embedded issues of fear regarding money that I grew up with. In fact, if it wasn't for his stability of character and support through my learning curves, I am sure it would have taken me much longer to trust God in this area. Being around people who have victory over what you are going through helps the process immensely. I no longer felt perplexed or confused at what was going on and I began to co-operate with the Holy Spirit and enjoy the ride.

Now it is your turn to craft a throne room prayer. There is a warning that goes along with this: Be ready for Him to use the ordinary and everyday circumstances of your life to bring about your transformation. He may use difficult relationships, undesirable circumstances, financial crisis, rejection, perfectionism or all of the above. It doesn't matter what He chooses to use, just recognize what it is and learn to co-operate with Him.

Exercise 3

**This exercise is taken in part from
Becoming the Beloved CD by
Graham Cooke.**

Consider a problem you are going through
right now (it doesn't matter how big or small).
Imagine yourself sitting off to the side in a room
while you watch Jesus and the Father at a table
having a conversation about you. What are you
hearing from that conversation? What are they
saying about what is going on in this particular
instance in your life? Take some time to journal
the conversation, using the notes section in the
back of this book.

It is okay if this feels silly. God will use silly
things to confound us and to help us grow up in
Him. Now take those notes and begin to write
three to six sentences that agree with what the
Father is showing you, or what the Father is
doing in your life. Thank Him for what He is
doing. This is your first throne room prayer.

I encourage you to write out prayers that agree with the Father.
Then read them out loud, over and over again. Faith comes
by hearing, and hearing, and hearing. Don't make them too

long, because I want you to memorize them. Keep them to the point, short and simple. Make sure you commit them to memory; after all you are co-operating with the Father in bringing heaven to earth.

CHAPTER 7

Praying in the Miraculous

"Most assuredly, I say to you, he who believes in
Me, the works that I do he will do also and
greater works than these he will do,
because I go to My Father."
John 14:12

We must remember that the miraculous and the supernatural are natural to God. It is only seen as miraculous to an un-renewed mind. We must also remember that we are not praying in the miraculous just to see signs, miracles, and wonders. There is a purpose behind all that the Father does. We need to agree with Him and His purpose, not our own agenda. As we spend more time in His presence we begin to see the reality of the purposes of heaven as more real than the reality we see with our natural eyes.

One of the things that will improve your ability to pray in, what we consider to be the miraculous, is to understand the difference between visitation and habitation. I will attempt to explain the difference here. As we are moving and learning to be all things in Christ, initially we may feel that we must take time to come aside and visit with the Father. This is our time of deep meditation on the things of the Lord, where we seek guidance, or an understanding of the meanings behind our dreams, or just to be filled with His peace. We may read scripture, study, pray, and worship. We are filling up our tank so that we can get on with our day without killing anyone. Just kidding.

So we go out into the world, and hope that the time we just spent with the Lord was enough to keep us going until our next visit with Him. However, when we begin to take what He is showing us during our time of visitation, and start to apply this wisdom to our everyday circumstances, we are learning the lesson of abiding. As we learn to abide in Him, we begin to take Him with us throughout the day. We learn to walk with Him, like two friends taking a stroll together all throughout the day. We find that as the day progresses we begin to see more things from His perspective. Over time, our perspective enlarges and things that seemed impossible begin to seem not so impossible.

That is the process of training for reigning. We are training ourselves to perceive kingdom reality. As this truth begins to usurp all of our past negative experiences and beliefs, we will begin to see signs, miracles, and wonders follow us.

I believe it is a deep work to be done for most of us because we have to be hungry for it. Oftentimes the Father will hide treasures from us because without doing the work of seeking the deeper revelation, we may not fully value the treasure.

The miraculous transforms lives. It not only transforms the lives of those touched in the case of a healing or creative miracle. It also has the capacity to transform the lives of those who are a witness to it, or those that hear the testimony of it. The purpose of a miracle is to bring people into kingdom reality. Praying in the miraculous is designed for us to experience how we are known in heaven. The soul also prospers when we pray in this way, because it is an eternal fix to a temporal problem. God is concerned with our eternal being. The miraculous is a place where our temporal being can meet up with our eternal being in the natural.

There is so much more that praying in the miraculous is able to do, than just meeting a perceived urgent need. The inner work to be done to come to this level of inner witness, is not work, for the sake of work. Each level of faith you pass through to attain this level of glory will impart revelation on how to move even closer and closer to the heart of the Father. Nothing is wasted as you dig deep into your everyday experiences, learning to see the miraculous works He is doing in your own spirit. As you learn how to carry that mantle within your own being, praying in the miraculous will be something you view as your rightly inheritance—signed, sealed and delivered.

While writing this chapter on the miraculous, the Father gave me a teaching. It was a very distinct message about the Kingdom of Heaven and how we should be able to expect the miraculous as members of His family. I kept hearing over and over again, "The Kingdom of Heaven is at hand, the Kingdom of Heaven is here; it is inside of you and wherever you are is where kingdom is. Wherever your feet tread, there is kingdom."

You have every right to expect the miraculous because the miraculous is part of the kingdom, and you are the kingdom. He said to me, "Once my people really begin to believe this, they will come to see the miraculous as their inheritance. They will come expectantly to the throne with a full and undivided heart and mind, demanding the seas to calm and the mountains to move. All of nature and its natural laws must bow down to the King of glory." The King has given us permission to upset the laws of nature and bring kingdom reality to earth. Let's get to work!

Appendix A

My Identity Statements

1. I am and I have more than enough, an overflow, an abundance of whatever is needed at the time.

2. I am content and grateful for what God has given me. I am happy with my portion.

3. I am full of mercy.

4. I am full of compassion and acceptance of God's people.

5. I am confident in the promises that God has made, and I am confident of who I am in Christ and in the heavenlies - warrior princess

6. I am full of God's love for Him, His people and myself.

7. I expect good things and the favor of God to be on my life.

8. I am kind.

9. I exhort and encourage your people.

10. I forgive, just as you forgave me.

11. I am full of your grace.

12. I expect success and embrace it. Any perceived failure is an opportunity in disguise.

13. I know who I am in Christ.

14. I am worthy, called by God before the foundations of this world.

15. I am effective in my ministry and in my work, and my prayer life.

16. I remain humble.

17. If I boast it is only in the Lord.

18. I am full of praise.

19. I am significant in Christ; I have my place in the kingdom.

20. I have a heart to reconcile God's people back to Him.

21. I am sober-minded, not thinking too highly of myself.

22. I am the be-loved of Christ.

23. I am accepted, adopted, chosen and grafted in.

24. I am full of His goodness.

25. I am the salt and light of the world.

26. I am sin-less: a new creature.

27. I am pure in heart.

28. I am rich.

29. I am victorious.

30. I am healed.

31. I am whole.

32. I am filled with vigor, vitality, youth and passion.

33. I am at ease. He makes everything easy. His yoke is easy and his burden is light.

34. I rest in Him.

35. I am at peace. He gives me that peace beyond all understanding.

36. I am patient.

37. I am steadfast in spirit and in heart.

38. I am confident.

39. I believe in the Christ.

40. I am faithful with what he has given me.

41. I am full of His joy!

Appendix B

Sample Throne Room Prayers

Kingdom Assignment Prayer

Thank You God that You give me this assignment to defeat the enemy's plots and plans against Your people.

Thank You, for giving me the ability to see the schemes of the enemy, and the permission and authority to tear down strongholds and repair broken hearts and mindsets, which set captives free.

Thank You, for anointing me to bring The Good News to prisoners.

Thank You, for allowing all to see your majesty through my life.

Thank You Lord for giving me the wisdom, knowledge and understanding to defeat your enemy at every turn in every arena.

Thank You, for giving me Your rest, Your blessed assurance, Your peace and Your joy, as I do battle for the kingdom!

Thank You, that You remind me that I fight from victory to victory!

<u>Prayer for Business</u>

Father, I thank You for this business You have given me.

I thank You that You have given me a market in which to do ministry in this land.

I thank and praise You that You teach me to pray for my customers, my co-workers and my company.

Thank You that You are the head of this ministry and out of it flows living waters, blessings, and prosperity.

But most of all I thank You for allowing it to be a vehicle for wealth transfer into the kingdom of God!

Amen

Prayer For the Miraculous

(This prayer was written for my niece London Reese Lawrence. Please join us in believing for a miracle in her life!)

Father, we thank You that You are a miracle-working God! Your Son, our Lord and Savior, paid the price for all illness and diseases.

We thank You that You are faithful and intentional to heal.

You are the truth that changes facts.

We declare London to be on earth as she is in heaven, strong, whole, and healed from any and all physical diseases, defects and abnormalities.

We declare that she is full of Your joy, peace, wisdom, understanding and love.

We thank You for the wisdom that You give her parents, to know the hope of Your glory in Christ Jesus.

We thank You that we see London, as You see London, completely and fully 100% healed.

We thank You for what You have already done in her life and how You continue to baffle the medical community through her complete restoration, even down to the DNA.

We love how You chose to show Your glory, power, and dominion through our London!

We will continue to give You all the honor, and all the glory and all the praise from now and forevermore.

Amen!

Prayer for Church Family

Thank You, Father, that you give us leaders that hear You and obey, no matter the cost.

Thank You that You continue to undergird our leaders with Your loving-kindness and protection.

Thank You that Your majesty overwhelms and empowers them to rapidly advance Your kingdom agenda, and Your goodness moves them above all circumstances.

Thank You that Your joy shatters all limitations and Your peace lives in them.

Thank You that You see us as a community of much-loved sons and daughters!

We declare the invasion of:

- Eyes to see and ears to hear the greatness of the Good News
- Acceleration into a fresh kingdom relationship and adventure
- A response to God's invitation for kingdom greatness
- Permission granted to explore new possibilities
- Follow-through with breakthrough
- A divine spirit of joyful encounter
- Encounters that go beyond knowledge
- Rest as warfare

Cited References

All scripture quotations unless otherwise indicated are taken from the *New King James Version* Copyright ©1979,1980,1982 by Thomas Nelson, Inc. Used by permission. All rights reserved.

Other versions used are:
The Amplified Bible copyright ©1958,1987 by the Lockman Foundation. Used by permission.

Chapter 1 What is Throne Room Prayer?

1. Graham Cooke, *Living your Truest Identity* (Brilliant Book House LLC 2012) 3 CD set. www.brilliantbookhouse.com

Chapter 5 How to make your prayers more effective

1. Stephen DeSilva, *Money and the Prosperous Soul* (Baker Publishing Group 2010) Kindle version location 254.

Chapter 6 Jesus as our Intercessor

1. Graham Cooke, *Becoming the Beloved* (Brilliant Book House LLC 2010) Devotional Soaking Series- Part 1 www.brilliantbookhouse.com

Notes

Notes